HODDESDON'S PAST
IN PICTURES

HODDESDON'S PAST IN PICTURES

by

David Dent

The Rockingham Press
1992

First published 1992
by The Rockingham Press
11 Musley Lane,
Ware, Herts SG12 7EN

**A catalogue record for this book is available
from the British Library**

ISBN 1 873468 08 3

Printed in Great Britain by
Biddles Limited
Guildford

**Part of the proceeds of this book are donated to
the Friends of Lowewood Museum, Hoddesdon**

Contents

The advertisements on the end papers of this book are from the programme for the Hoddesdon Swimming Club Gala held at the Brewery Baths, Bell Lane in 1926 - see page 144.

Acknowledgements

It was never my intention to devote so much time to studying Hoddesdon's past, as I have always been equally interested in the history of the villages of Broxbourne and Wormley. However, following some friendly persuasion from fellow members of the Hoddesdon Society I decided to focus my attention on the town. As I began my research, I realised how great a debt I owed to Messrs. Tregelles, Hayllar and Paddick, whose earlier histories of Hoddesdon made my task much easier.

The majority of illustrations in this book are from my own collection of old postcards and photographs, which I have acquired over the past fifteen years. Many have subsequently been transferred to slide, and I have spent many enjoyable evenings sharing the collection with local groups and organisations - and learning a great deal more about the town in the process. However, this book would not have been possible without the help and encouragement of other people. I would like to thank my family, especially my wife Margaret, for all their help. My thanks go also to Sue Garside for kindly offering to undertake the onerous task of proof reading and, last but by no means least, I must thank David Perman for agreeing to publish this book and for his help and interest throughout.

I must also acknowledge the very many people who have lent me photographs during the last fifteen years and, in mentioning their names, I apologise if I have left anyone out: Mr. Neil Jenkins, Mr. Reg Head, Mr. D. Hale, the late Mr. J. Mortimer, Mrs. J. Whitelegg, Mrs. M. Fletcher, Mrs. J. Brown, Mrs. Malyon, Mrs. Bradshaw, Mrs. R. Swallow, Miss E. Treble, Dr. A. Barclay, Mrs. P. Barclay, Mr. D. Parsons, Mr. P. Manning, Mr. Welch, Mrs. Golledge, Mrs. Paddick, Mr. Porter, Mr. E. Walsh, Mr. P. Rooke, Mr. L. Dent, Mrs. R. Noton, Mr. G. Hoade, Mrs. Leslie, Mr. Burton, Tom Doig and the staff of Lowewood Museum, and Jean Holmes and Jack Wetherill and the staff of Hoddesdon Library.

I am also grateful to the Enfield and St. Albans Cooperative Society for permission to use the photograph on page 52 which is their Copyright, and to the Royal Commission on the Historical Monuments of England for permission to use their Copyright photographs on pages 85, 86, 87, 107, and the bottom photograph on page 106, all from the National Buildings Record.

The accuracy of the facts in this book have been checked as carefully as possible. However, original sources can contain errors and memories fade. Please contact the author if you have any further information or would be prepared to lend original photographs for copying and possible display at Lowewood Museum.

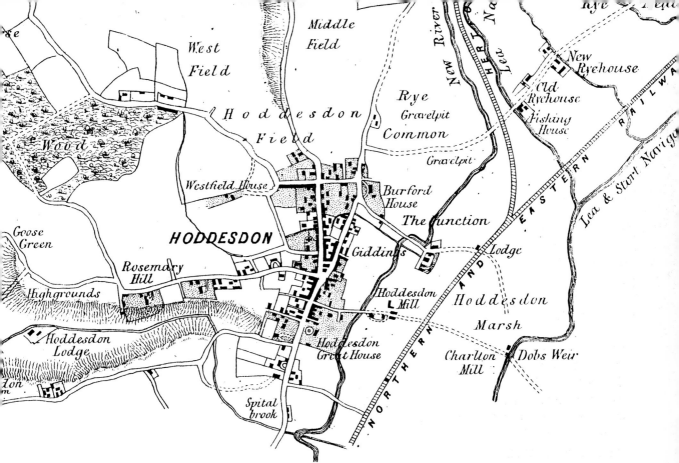

Part of the map of Hoddesdon from the Public Health Report of 1851.

Introduction

The town of Hoddesdon has changed quite dramatically in the past 30 years. This process has seen the demolition of a number of buildings of historical and architectural importance, and the disappearance of a number of well-known shops and local businesses. Sadly many of the so-called "improvements" of the 1960's were not successful, and we have been left with the legacy of what the planners of the time thought was the way forward.

Despite the changes, Hoddesdon still retains interesting buildings, as well as traces of its medieval origins in the form of its street plan, which is that of an undefended market town with tenements either side of a single main street. Hoddesdon was granted a charter for a market and fair in 1253, and at one time it had a market cross, and later a market hall.

The town prospered and grew through the centuries, although any new buildings tended to be constructed alongside the main thoroughfare, and its two northern arteries, Amwell Street and Burford Street. This is shown very clearly by the map of 1851.

The illustrations in this book span nearly two hundred years. They cover a range of subjects, but they can only give the reader a small glimpse of the town's past. I am indebted to many fine photographers for providing me with a record of days gone by, and I am left to ponder upon what gems we might be privy to had the art of photography been invented a hundred years earlier.

This unusual building was known as "Braithwaite's Castle". It was, in fact, a Gothic-style lodge built in about 1830 for John Warner's Woodlands Estate.

Southern Approaches

Our journey starts at the southern end of the town where Spitalbrook passes under the road. Until the 18th century all traffic passing this point would have had to ford the brook. No actual date for the construction of the first bridge is known, but in 1835 it was recorded in the highway sessions papers that the bridge was 'much out of repayre'.

A hospital, first mentioned in 1390, once stood to the east of the road. It may at one time have been used by lepers, but by the 16th century it was being used as a hospital for sick and infirm old people, and had assumed the status of almshouses. By 1583 it had closed, and the buildings had been taken over by the Free Grammar School, which was established under charter from Queen Elizabeth I in 1560. The school did not prosper and was closed in 1595.

Sometime after 1840 the Cheshunt Turnpike Trust moved their Hoddesdon tollgate to a point close by Spitalbrook bridge, and also built a toll-house. These were both removed in 1872.

SPITAL BROOK, BROXBOURNE.

(Above) A postcard of circa 1908 showing Spitalbrook.   On the right is The George which was built in about 1860.
(Below) Spitalbrook looking south towards Broxbourne in about 1905.

HODDESDON, ADMIRALS WALK

(Above) Admiral's Walk, seen from the bank of the New River, in about 1940. The development of housing in this area began in 1884. It took its name from Admiral Donat Henchy O'Brien who lived in Yew House in the High Street from 1832 until his death in 1857. As the name suggests, he often walked this area armed with his gun and accompanied by his dogs.

(Below) The bridge over the New River at Admiral's Walk in around 1905. Work began on this man-made waterway in 1609 and it was completed in 1613. It originally ran from Chadwell Spring outside Ware to Clerkenwell, to provide the City of London with drinking water.

(Above) The entrance to Holly Walk, circa 1910. This is the footpath which runs from Upper Marsh lane to St. Catherine's Estate.

(Below) The house on the right of this picture is Harteshorne, which was at one time an inn known as the "Five Bells". Just beyond it can be seen the entrance to Yewlands Estate, which was developed in 1908.

The High Street circa 1905. The iron pump replaced the statue of the Samaritan woman in 1826. The pump itself was removed after being badly damaged by a car driven by Viscount Gladstone's chauffeur.

The High Street

The High Street is a long ribbon of development which runs from Upper Marsh Lane to the Clock Tower. At one time, there was a clear distinction between commercial properties situated at the northern end of the street and the large private houses which ran south from Esdale Lane. The line of the road has remained virtually unaltered for centuries, but many of the buildings that once graced it have been demolished.

As one looks at the tarmac and paving of today, it is difficult to imagine the habit of earlier inhabitants of throwing "litter" on to the highway to be trodden in, and then removing it to provide a top dressing for their land. Towards the end of the 17th century, this was causing so much damage to the road that a special order was passed requiring two loads of gravel to be laid down for each load of manure taken away. Failure to comply with this order incurred a penalty of 2s.6d. for every load.

Elm Place and Yew House, Hoddesdon.

(Above) Elm Place on the left of the picture was another building which was once an inn. Like many inns in the town, it once brewed its own beer and the brewing apparatus was still intact late in the 19th century.
(Below) The junction of Cock Lane and the High Street circa 1908.

High Street. Hoddesdon.

(Above) The High Street, looking south, in 1955. On the right is the building which housed the town's first Woolworth store.
(Below) The High Street, looking north, in 1910. On the right is Rathmore House built in 1743.

(Above) The High Street looking south, in about 1905. John Loudon McAdam, "the great improver of British roads", lived in the second house on the left from 1825-1836.   Known as Montague House, its ground floor is now the banking hall of Lloyds Bank.
(Below) The High Street at its junction with Conduit Lane circa 1935.   Inscribed on the back of this postcard is the description "Grande Rue d' Hoddesdon".

This superb view of the High Street was taken on the 18th June 1902. This was a Wednesday and Market Day. In the background, it is just possible to see the livestock pens. The photograph itself was taken by Mr. Alfred Burton, a well-known local photographer, who had a studio in Roman Street. The business was taken over in 1913 by Mr. Burton's son, Charles, and carried on until about 1951.

Town Hall, Hoddesdon.

(Above) The Clock Tower was built on the site of the old Chapel of St. Katherine in 1836. Although it was referred to as the "Town Hall", it was quite inadequate for that purpose. However, it did contain a vestry room at the front, a room at the back for the horse-drawn fire engine, living and sleeping accommodation for the town constable and cells for prisoners.
(Below) A view from the high pavement at the top of Amwell Street in the late 1930's.

HODDESDON.
"FROM THE RISE."
82789.

"HAVEN'T YOU ANY JAFFA ORANGES?"
"NONE JAFFER THAN THEM, LADY, BUT YOU'D BE SURPRISED HOW JAFF THEY ARE."

When the humorous magazine "Punch" wished to portray the English middle classes between the wars, it came to Hoddesdon. The familiar landmarks of the Bull Hotel and the Clock Tower are featured in these two cartoons. The one above appeared in the issue of the 20th June 1928, followed by that below in the issue of the 13th September 1933.

Society Leader (discussing new-comers).
"QUITE COMMON PEOPLE, I
SHOULD THINK, MY DEAR.
THEY TAKE THEIR HOLIDAYS IN
AUGUST."

This superb aerial view of Hoddesdon was taken in 1962 by Bishop Marshall. It captures the centre of the town just before it was devastated by the wholesale changes of 1964. The building with the large garden in the bottom right of the picture was Amwell House. Towards the top of the picture can be seen an area of glasshouses, which belonged to Mr. Gocher the butcher. These were removed when the development of Fawkon Walk began.

Amwell Street, looking north in about 1900.

Amwell and Burford Streets

In earlier times, Amwell and Burford Streets were known as Ware Valley and Stanstead Valley respectively.

During the latter half of the 19th century, Amwell Street was well served by a number of inns and drinking houses. On the western side were the Old Harrow, the Sun, the Queen's Head and the Crown, and on the eastern side the Duncombe Arms, the Victoria, the Vine and the Rose and Crown. Today the original line of the northern end of the street acts only as a service road. Properties on the western side were demolished in 1973 to make way for a new road system.

Burford Street was also altered by the new road scheme, and also lost a number of buildings, including the Five Horseshoes pub which stood on the site of the old Broxbourne Parish Workhouse.

However, things could have been far worse. In 1951, a leaflet was published to show the projected growth of Hoddesdon up to 1973; it also showed the North Orbital Road (the forerunner of the M25) passing over Amwell and Burford Streets on a viaduct!

(Above) *Amwell Street, looking south in around 1910. The horse-drawn vehicle on the right hand side of the road is a Hoddesdon Urban District Council road sweeper's cart. Three pub signs are visible in the picture: on the right are the signs of the Crown and the Queen's Head, with the Rose and Crown on the left.*

(Below) *The Fourways was the point where Hertford Road, Ware Road, Duke Street and Amwell Street all converged. Fourways House in the background was a small Georgian town house, built in about 1760.*

This view of the town end of Amwell Street dates from the turn of the century. Before 1826, the drop down into "Ware Valley" was much steeper, but in that year the gradient was reduced under the direction of James Loudon McAdam. As a result of this the town gained the distinctive feature of Amwell Street's high pavement.

(Above) Burford Street at the junction with Roman Street, looking south towards the town.

(Left) The building in this photograph was secured on a lease by Broxbourne Parish Council in 1737 for use as a workhouse. The first Master was a John Fisher who along with his wife agreed to live at the workhouse and keep and take care of the poor for a fee of 1s. 6d. per head, with a reasonable fee added in case of smallpox.

A view of Ware Road, looking north, in about 1910. On the left is Geneva House which stood next to New Farm. Note the absence of buildings on the right-hand side of the road.

Northern Approaches

From the north, Hoddesdon is approached by way of Stanstead Road, Ware Road or Hertford Road. Before the First World War, these roads were devoid of any major housing development. However, since that time there has been a great deal of building, starting in the 1920's with ribbon development, followed by widespread infilling. More recently, large estates have been developed between Ware Road and Stanstead Road. These were built mainly on the sites of former market gardens, the largest being the Hundred Acre Estate where the first houses were completed in 1968.

(Above) Hertford Road looking down the hill towards Fourways in about 1910. In 1470, this was known as Foxtons Lane.

(Below) Stanstead Road at its junction with Rye Road. On the left is the old pond which was filled in in 1954, and beyond it is Pound Close, which probably took its name from the pound of the Manor of Geddings. A pound was a pen where stray animals were placed.

The police station in Lord Street was opened in 1883. Before then the town's constables had been housed in the building around the base of the Clock Tower.

Western Approaches

From the west, Hoddesdon is approached by two roads of secondary importance. The first of these is Lord Street or Lord's Lane, so called because it may well have led to the Manor House of Richard de Boxe which stood a little to the west of High Leigh.

The second road is Cock Lane at the southern end of the High Street. It was not a major route of any kind and was for many centuries just an old green track leading to woodland to the west of the town. It took its name from the Cock Inn, which stood on the site of the Grange.

Brocket Road which joins the High Street in the centre of the town was originally only an accommodation lane leading to Lowfield.

(Above) Lord Street at the junction with Rosevale, circa 1910.

(Bottom) A view down Lord Street, looking towards the town.   On the left is a very old timber-framed building, with an unusual roof structure.

(Above) Rosevale leading on to Parkview was formerly a cart track joining Lord Street and Cock Lane. However, towards the end of the 19th century a number of large villas were built along it.

(Below) The old ford across the Spitalbrook in Cock Lane in a photograph of about 1910.

The Brook, Grange Lane, Hoddesdon.

Old Highway at its junction with Haward Road in about 1905.

Rye Park

At the beginning of the 19th century, Rye Park as we know it today was virtually devoid of housing, being known as Ryefield or Rye Common. However, the Enclosures Act of 1855 allowed large fields to be divided and enclosed, and as a result more land became available for building. Charles Whitley Junior was very much involved in this process, and from the late 1870's housing development of the old Rye Common area began. One thing the Victorians were quite good at was dating their houses, and in this respect it is possible to trace the development of Rye Park by looking out for dating plaques on the houses in Whitley Road, Walton Road, the Old Highway and Rumbold Road. At the western end of Rye Road, the first council houses were built in 1921. By 1950, Rye Park had become the most populous single area in the Urban District of Hoddesdon.

(Above) Rye Road looking west in the late 1930's. Old Highway is on the right.
(Bottom) The shops in Rye Road date from the early 1930's. The Rye Road Electric Bakery, J. Moore & Sons' boot and shoe shop and the Handy Stores all feature prominently on this postcard.

Dobbs Weir Lock on the Lea Navigation in around 1905.

Dobbs Weir

Although Essex is very close to Hoddesdon, in former times there was very little communication between the town and the adjoining country due to the absence of bridges.

At Dobbs Weir, there was a ford, but the first mention of a bridge does not occur until 1604, when James I's Council instructed Sir Robert Wroth and others "to forward the making of bridges over the River Lee between Hackney and Hoddesdon for the greater convenience of the King when hawking". It is fairly certain that a bridge was built, and probably stood on or close to the site of the present concrete bridge, which was constructed in 1935.

(Above) The Fish and Eels was a popular Victorian riverside inn. Its most notorious publican was the Revd. Samuel Thackeray. When he applied for the tenancy in 1906, he was dismissed from his chaplaincy at the Gordon Road Workhouse in Camberwell, whereupon he held services in the Fish and Eels' bar.
(Below) Another view of the pub from the banks of the Lea Navigation in circa 1910.

THE OLD MARKET HOUSE, HODDESDON, HERTS
Taken during the General Election 1832.

Drawn, Etched & Published by Charles Warren, 13, Thistle Grove, Little Chelsea

An etching of the Market House, made at the time of the Reform Bill Election in 1832.   Erected in 1634, the Market House was 50 feet long and 40 feet wide.

Markets and Fairs

In 1253, Richard de Boxe, who held the small manor of Boxe in Hoddesdon, was given a Royal Grant from Henry III to hold a market on Thursday of each week. Little is known of Richard de Boxe but he must have been a man of some influence and wealth to obtain such a grant for Hoddesdon, which at that time was only a small hamlet containing few houses.

From about 1460 onwards the bailiffs of Hertford made many attempts to close down the Hoddesdon market, claiming that Henry VI - who in his early days lived at Hertford Castle - had granted that town the right to hold a weekly market to the exclusion of any others within a seven mile radius. The dispute was not settled until 1560 when Hoddesdon's right to hold a weekly market was upheld.

The market grew with the increase of traffic through the town and before the end of the 16th century it was famous for its dealings in malt. In the rental accounts of 1571, there is a list of 28 market stalls and the yearly rent of each was 4d. to the manor, with a "fine" of either eight shillings or ten shillings on the sale or transfer of the stall. Even the side and end walls of the Chapel of St. Katherine were used for lean-to stalls and shops.   In 1596, there was much complaint that the improved navigation of the River Lee was causing much of the malt to be carried past the town by barges. This would certainly have affected the market, and from this point it suffered a steady decline in its fortunes.

The Market House and the Bull face each other across the street in this drawing by Buckler, dated 1832. In the following year, the Market House was pulled down on the orders of the Marquess of Salisbury, who had received written representations from the people of Hoddesdon claiming that it was causing traffic congestion in the High Street.

The market regulations appear only in the Geddings Court Rolls, and they give us an insight into the hustle and bustle of the market as it was almost four hundred years ago. There would have been a gathering of a great variety of traders - maltsters, butchers, fishmongers, tanners, brewers, farmers and country people generally - the ground would have been unpaved and undrained, with stray pigs and cattle hindering the traffic in the narrow ways left by the stalls. An order of 1594 reads thus: "That all who suffer their hogges to go abroade in the street upon the market daye between nyne of the clocke in the morninge and three of the clocke in the afternoone to forfeit for every hogge 4d."

The Market House was erected in 1634 as one of the improvements promoted by Marmaduke Rawdon, who gave "fortie pounds towards the finishing of it". The market rallied for a time, but then the decay set in again and during the next two hundred years its importance to the town gradually declined. It finally petered out following the removal of the Market House in 1833.

The cattle and livestock market, started by Ernest Bridgeman, a local auctioneer, on the 24th March 1886, was a new venture and not a revival of the old market - although he had a yearly tenancy of the rights. The new market was held on Wednesdays and proved to be a great success. However, after the First World War, it became less popular and a few stalls occupied by outsiders began to be put up. This led to a petition by the local Traders' Association to the council, and after a considerable negotiation the latter finally acquired the market rights from the Marquess of Salisbury and the market, as we know it today, began to take shape.

(Above) Hoddesdon's new Wednesday livestock market, photographed on the day that it opened, the 24th March 1886.

(Below) The market in 1910 under the watchful eyes of the local constabulary

Hoddesdon, Market Place.

(Above) In this view of the market everything looks orderly, but most of the livestock was driven to market on the hoof and there were often some exciting chases when animals broke away. (Below) A typical market day in the 1950's. The livestock market ceased in about 1930, but general stalls had begun to appear during the 1920's.

HDSN. 24 HODDESDON, High Street

The market occupying its present position on a summer's day in 1935. The single-decker bus in the foreground is an early Green Line coach, which ran from Hertford to Byfleet.

This view of the remains of the fair in 1851 is the oldest photograph in this book. The dilapidated cottages in front of the Clock Tower were known as Middle Row and were pulled down in 1857.

Along with the Royal Grant for a market in 1253, Richard de Boxe was also granted the right to hold a fair on the Feast of St. Martin (11th November). In 1559, a charter from Queen Elizabeth I also allowed a fair to be held on the Feast of St. Peter (29th June) and the two following days. The former fair had been abandoned long ago. The fair was originally based upon commercial concerns, such as the sale of horses and livestock, but later changed its purpose to one of pleasure. For centuries, it was held in the main street and continued until the last decade of the 19th century when the noise and crowds became a nuisance. It was then moved to a field in Amwell Street, near where the old Sun Public House stood, and then to Pound Close, which is still visited each year by a funfair.

An aerial view of Christie's Brewery in around 1920. When it was bought in 1928 by the Cannon Brewery of Clerkenwell in London, the new owners pulled down parts of the brewery and sold off other buildings. It is still possible to see some of Christie's old buildings in Brewery Road, all used for different purposes than those for which they were built.

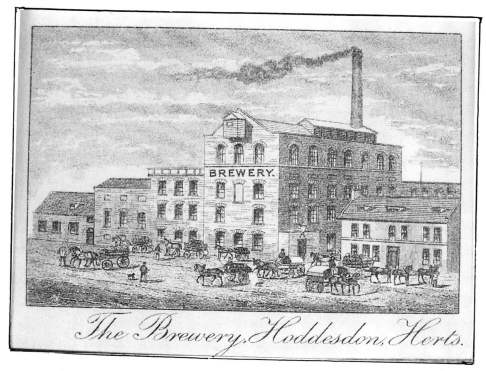

The letterhead on the official stationery of Christie's Brewery.

Brewing

At one time each inn in the town brewed its own ale, but the first mention of a brewery appears in notes relating to the perambulation of the parish boundaries in 1736. This was the brewhouse of Robert Plomer who built it into a thriving business after he inherited it from his father William in 1728. Robert became a rich and influential man and was at one time High Sheriff of Hertfordshire.

In 1803, William Christie and George Cathrow acquired the brewery from the Whittingstall family who had owned it since 1781. The brewery was known as Christie and Cathrow even after William's death in 1811, and continued to flourish until 1842 when George Cathrow died. The brewery premises and inns were then purchased by John Back and Robert Hunt who took into partnership Peter Christie, William's nephew. They also purchased John Moses Carter's brewery in St. Andrew's Street, Hertford, which was closed and its 40-odd pubs were added to the Hoddesdon Brewery estate . The brewery at Hoddesdon was then completely rebuilt.

Robert Hunt retired in about 1860, Peter Christie died in 1865 and shortly afterwards John Back retired. The brewery then passed into the sole ownership of Peter's son, Charles Peter Christie, although it had operated as C.P. Christie and Co. since at least 1862. It remained in the ownership of the Christie family until it was sold to the Cannon Brewery of Clerkenwell in London and was officially handed over to them in April 1928. The new owners promptly closed the brewery and put the entire contents up for auction. Shortly afterwards, large parts of the Hoddesdon brewery were pulled down and other buildings were altered and sold off.

(Left) Charles Peter Christie, the son of Peter Christie and his wife Ellen Louisa (daughter of the Revd. William Jones, Vicar of Broxbourne) was sole owner of the Hoddesdon Brewery from 1865 until his death in 1898. He was a great benefactor of the town, but a formidable business-man who made many additions and improvements to the Hoddesdon Brewery until it was the fourth largest in the county. He also took great pride in the brewery's horses and instructed his carters and draymen to walk at their horses' heads for the first mile out of town and the last mile in.

After C.P. Christie's death, the brewery was run as a partnership by his four sons until the founding of a private company in 1903. At that time, Christie's owned 124 pubs and beerhouses in Hertfordshire alone, including 16 out of 24 in Hoddesdon itself. However, the fortunes of the family and the company suffered a serious set-back when a disastrous fire broke out in the early hours of Tuesday 3rd January 1905. It destroyed the brewery's No. 1 Malting and seriously damaged No. 2, as well as some ancillary buildings. The fire was tackled by the brewery's own brigade as well as those from the town and from Ware, but the damage was estimated at £10,000. After the First World War, there were further problems when a yeast infection got into the beer and proved difficult to eradicate. Finally, following the suicide of Captain John Christie, who had suffered terribly from a head wound received in the trenches in 1915, it was decided to sell the brewery. It was first offered to McMullen's of Hertford who turned it down and then to the Cannon Brewery of London, who purchased it in 1928.

Brewery waggons parading for Mr. Charles Peter Christie before the traditional Whit Monday display of all the local breweries on Hartham Common, Hertford.

For a number of years preceding C.P. Christie's death in 1898, there was great excitement in the town on Whit Monday mornings. At about 10 o'clock, Mr. Christie would arrive with his sons to inspect the brewery vehicles, which were gathered on the triangle of land in front of the Clock House. The whole parade was subjected to a rigorous inspection and nothing was missed. By the time the inspection had finished, a great crowd of townspeople would have gathered to watch the turn out. When the inspection was completed, the parade wheeled to the right and set off down Amwell Street towards Hertford. In the 1890's, Christie's most popular beer was dold for one shilling a gallon.

Another view of C.P. Christie with some of the men who would have arrived at 5 a.m. to prepare the cards, drays and vans for the Whit Monday parade.

(Above) The brewery stables were rebuilt in 1889 and this photograph was taken shortly after their completion.

(Below) A Christie's dray being inspected by C.P. Christie on Whit Monday 1895.

(Above) Fire was a constant danger in the malting process and the Hoddesdon Brewery had its own fire brigade. The brewery suffered as a result of the fire of 1905.
(Below) Three of Christie's draymen in 1923. The man in the middle is Mr. "Topper" Fountain.

A good supply of pure water is essential for the brewing process and Christie's was fortunate in having its own well which produced excellent water. This photograph shows the pump house, with a new pump being put through its paces.

The Bull Hotel in about 1900. It first appears in the town's record in 1578, when John Squyer the landlord was reported to Lord Burghley for allowing it to be used by persons known to have been in contact with the plague, which was then raging in London.

Inns and Pubs

By the 15th century there were three main types of licensed premises: alehouses or beerhouses, which brewed their own beer or ale on the premises but provided no food or lodging, inns which provided shelter and stabling of horses as well as food and drink, and finally taverns where wine was sold and food and drink provided.

In 1630, two Hoddesdon alehouse keepers found themselves in trouble with the authorities: "there is a presentment that Thomas Luth of Hodson, in the Parish of Broxbourne, kept evil rule in his house, and allowed unknown men to be drunk there" and "William Allen, alehouse keeper of the same town, who permitted one William Slaten and others to be drunk in his house". Unfortunately, we do not know which establishments these alehouse keepers were connected with.

From about 1790 until the 1840's, most of Hoddesdon's inns and pubs would have been kept busy by the 27 coaches and four mail coaches which came to, or passed through, the town daily. Even after the decline of coaching with the coming of the railway, we still find that in 1860 "there were 36 inns and five beerhouses in the town at that time, and they were open from 6 a.m. until midnight". A number of interesting public houses, which were formerly inns, still survive in the town, namely the Golden Lion, the White Swan, the Salisbury Arms and the Bell.

(Above) The fame of the Bull was spread wide in the early 18th century when the Essex poet, Matthew Prior, devoted eleven verses of his poem "Down Hall" to the inn, its landlady and her staff.

(Below) The Salisbury Arms was re-fronted in the 18th century. Before 1826 it was known as the "Black Lyon".

(Above) The White Swan circa 1900 when it was just "The Swan". The main parts of the building are timber-framed dating from the 16th century.
(Below) In the Hertfordshire volume of his "Buildings of England", Nicholas Pevsner described the White Swan as "visually the most striking timber-framed inn in the district". Before 1963, the northern end of the building was a shop.

The Maidenhead was first mentioned as an inn in 1576. In 1742 and probably earlier, it had its own malting. The inn was acquired by Christie and Cathrow in 1825 and, like most of the large inns in the town, had stabling for a number of horses.

(Above) A postcard view of the High Street showing the Golden Lion in around 1910.   Parts of this inn date from the late 16th century.
(Below) In 1756 the Bell had stabling for 20 horses. In this picture, 150 years later, it was catering for a different kind of traveller and offering accommodation for cyclists.

(Above) An outing from the Sun public house in Amwell Street in 1936.

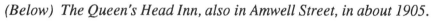

(Below) The Queen's Head Inn, also in Amwell Street, in about 1905.

(Above)   The Five Horseshoes in Burford Street was built on the site of the Broxbourne Parish Workhouse (see page 24) in 1866.   It was demolished in the early 1970's as part of the clearance for the Dinant Relief Road.
(Below) The Star in Burford Street was closed on the 4th July 1972 and demolished - again to make way for the Relief Road.

(Above) The Old Highway Tavern was built towards the end of the 19th century, when the Rye Park area of the town was developed.
(Below) Celebrations outside the Boar's Head on the occasion of George V's Silver Jubilee in 1935. The earliest mention of this public house is 1756, when troops were billetted here.

(Above) Before 1745 this inn was known as the Peahen, but the name was changed in honour of *Duke William of Cumberland* who in that year marched his troops through the town on their way to Scotland.

(Below) The Coffee or Three Cups Tavern was built in 1882 in an attempt to wean the townspeople away from alcohol. But, even as late as 1898, there was one public house for every 127 people in Hertfordshire and the number of cases of drunkenness was high.

The new Enfield Highway Cooperative store in Amwell Street was opened in 1915, with departments for groceries and provisions, clothing, drapery and boots and shoes.

Shops and Shopkeepers

Hoddesdon has always had an interesting mix of shops, but changes in shopping habits have left the town - except for a few notable survivors - devoid of the choice and variety which was once so abundant.

The shops of today owe much to our Victorian forefathers who had to cope with an expansion of consumption in the latter part of the 19th century. Having catered largely for the middle class, the Victorian shopkeeper found that they were playing an increasingly important role in the lives of the working class. This new role was mainly in the area of food supply, and it led to the growth of multiple-stores such as the Home and Colonial and International Stores, both of which had branches in the town.

At the turn of the century, most shops were open for twelve hours a day, six days a week. Late night shopping is not an invention of the present day.

(Above) The Hoddesdon Cooperative Society was started in 1868 but remained small, trading from one shop in Burford Street.

(Below) Hogges Hall, like many private houses in the centre of the town, was converted into shops. This view dates from 1935.

(Above) *Ashford's Stores, at 61 - 63 High Street, in about 1910. The picture shows, left to right, Mr. Brown, Mr. W. Ashford, Mr. F. Drane and Mr. J. Copping.*
(Below) *Another view of Ashford's Stores, which was taken over in 1949 by F.W. Wash and Son Ltd., who also had shops in Broxbourne and Wormley. In 1951 they acquired the northern end of the building from Mr. Brooks. The name was changed to Meadows in about 1960 when the shops became self-service.*

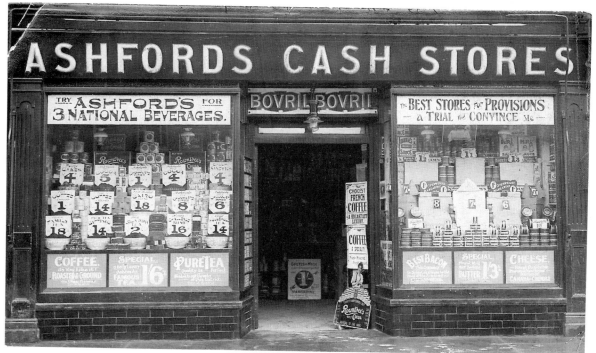

(Above) The White Heather Dairy was a short-lived business at 47 High Street, which is now occupied by Boots Opticians.

(Below) This photograph of the International Stores at 31 High Street dates from around 1905.

The author's maternal grandfather, Mr. Edward Hoade, owned this butcher's shop in Burford Street. Earlier he had a shop in Whitley Road. In 1935, the business moved to 25 High Road, Wormley. The picture shows, left to right, Ted Brown, Cecil Burt, T. Howard and, in the doorway, Mr. Hoade.

(Above) *Mr. C.E. Brooks outside his ironmonger's shop in the High Street, now part of Meadows'. When this photograph was taken in around 1910, Mr. Brooks was also the agent for Royal Enfield Cycles.*

(Below) *Mr. Newman ran his cycle depot from 101 Burford Street. This is not a postcard but an ink blotter, which also served as an advertisement.*

High Street, Hoddesdon.

This postcard view of the High Street, taken in about 1910, was one of a series produced and published by Mr. R.C. Mitchell. His stationer's shop, known as "the Hoddesdon Bazaar", can be seen on the right. It is a view of the High Street that is never likely to be repeated - with more cycles than either motor cars or horse-drawn vehicles.

The bicycle or velocipede, as it was at first called, was introduced into Britain in the 1860's. But the bicycle craze really took off in the 1890's with the invention of the pneumatic tyre. Many celebrities took up cycling, including H.G. Wells and Sir Arthur Conan Doyle and it soon became the best means for townspeople to explore the countryside. Many cycling clubs were formed and in 1899 there were 60,000 members of the Cyclists' Touring Club. Many of the North London clubs cycled out to the Hoddesdon area at weekends and the old coaching inns found new customers among the cyclists. Cycling, like tennis and archery, was a sport taken up by women and became a symbol of female emancipation. The increased popularity of cycling produced an increase in the number of cyclemakers and the 1901 Census revealed that their number had grown by 173% within ten years.

(Above) *The printing firm of Thomas Knight was founded in 1915 in premises behind what is now the gas showrooms, and in 1919 moved to 90 High Street, where it is shown here in the late 1920's. In 1930 it moved again to Brewery Road where it remained in business until 1980.*
(Below) *Brocket Stores, pictured here in 1960, was originally Nazeing Chapel, built in 1816. It became a shop, owned by Mr. William Hampton, in 1876 and later became the premises where Mr. E.D. Allen manufactured "Brocket Cycles".*

(Above) *Ashford's Estate Office on the corner of Brocket Road in about 1914 - the forerunner of the estate agents which are now a familiar feature of Hoddesdon High Street.*

(Below) *Shops on the corner of Conduit Lane circa 1912.*

(Above) Fordham & Company's furniture store in the early 1960's.

(Below) Mr. Douglas Fordham, third from the left, making a presentation to his staff in 1984 to celebrate the firm's 50 years of trading in the town. Fordham's closed in October 1987.

High Street, Hoddesdon.

Mitchell Series

This view of the High Street dates from about 1938. The shops on the left-hand side of the street are Gibson's, the Home and Colonial and the International Stores. This group of buildings was badly damaged on the night of the 10th May 1941, when a single enemy aircraft dropped some fourteen bombs in a line stretching from the Ware Road to the Hoddesdon U.D.C. offices.

The Wilsmore family ran this little sweet shop at 63 Burford Street. It was demolished in 1973.

Employees of the Hoddesdon Gas Company pictured in the 1890's. The Gas Company was formed in 1847 when street lighting was installed. To coincide with the first lighting of the gas lamps on Monday the 24th January 1848 a special dinner was arranged at the Salisbury Arms. However, at the appointed hour nothing happened, due to a problem with the piped gas supply. But the dinner went ahead regardless.

Hoddesdon at Work

From the middle of the 19th century until its closure in 1928 the Brewery was the largest employer in the town. However, in the 1890's, market-gardening under glass established itself in the upper Lea Valley. By 1950, glasshouses covered 320 acres of the old Hoddesdon Urban District, providing jobs for thirty per cent of the town's employed population.

The building industry has always provided work for the inhabitants of Hoddesdon, with firms such as J.A. Hunt Ltd., W.J. Haward, and Sams and Bryant involved in both local and national development projects.

In the years up to and following the Second World War, a variety of other businesses became established in the town. Firms such as Shockcrete, Nissen Buildings, Sharp and Dohme and the printers Thomas Knight and Company will be familiar names to those who have lived in the town for any length of time. Today, a large proportion of the working population commute to jobs outside the immediate area - by train and increasingly by car - although the development of new industrial estates, particularly in the Essex Road area, has provided many new jobs.

George Henry Porter standing at the entrance to the forge which stood in the High Street in the 1920's. With him is a horse called "Big Ben" from Christie's Brewery. Mr. Porter, who had previously worked as a farrier for Christie's and for the powder mills at Enfield, was the last blacksmith to use these premises which had been a smithy for over 200 years. The building is now occupied by Ripley, the butcher's, and the area of granite setts in the foreground of this picture still survives.

(Above) A photograph of the workmen who built St. Cuthbert's Church, Rye Park in 1908. They were employed by the Hoddesdon building firm of J.A. Hunt.
(Below) John Alfred Hunt took over control of the firm in 1869. This view shows some of the firm's workshops at the rear of Hogges Hall in the High Street.

(*Above*) *Another group of workmen outside Hunt's Brocket Road workshops in around 1905.*
(*Below*) *Parrott Brothers of Amwell Street carried out street cleaning for Hoddesdon Urban District Council for many years. This photograph shows their horse, Peggy, on her last working day.*

(Above and Below) The Gough Brothers in 1908 outside their wheelwrights' and coach-building premises, which adjoined the Coffee Tavern Hall in Lord Street.

Another example of the Gough Brothers' work - the horse-drawn van of an itinerant preacher, who offered "a bright Gospel Service".

Albert and Daniel Gough set up their coachbuilding, wheelwrights' and farriers' business in November 1904. Both had served their apprenticeships in North Devon, Albert as a blacksmith and Daniel as a coachbuilder. The business flourished until March 1925.

(Above and Below) Some of the staff in the bottling and packing department of Beltona, which was based at Amwell House, the home of Mr. Belton who produced and marketed the cure.

(Opposite) An advertisement in 1925 for the Beltona arthritis cure.

Mr. and Mrs. Belton (seated, third from the left and right) with the famous boxer Len Harvey and the Beltona staff, outside Amwell House. The patent arthritis cure was originally used as a hair lotion and embrocation in Mr. Belton's hairdressing business, where he noticed that it eased the arthritic condition in the fingers of one of his assistants. It was then tried on a well-known local character, Dicky Jaggs, whose legs were locked together by arthritis, and as a result he was able to walk a little. Later it was advertised as a rub for athletes and an advertisement was used featuring the boxer Len Harvey. It was then known as "Len Harvey's magic rub, which supples the muscles".

(Above) *Hoddesdon Fire Brigade in 1939. Back row (l to r): Gerry Parrott, Ron Fox, Les Newman, Johnny Gibbs, Jack Newport and George Cheek. Front row: Sid Ansell (Regular Fireman and Chief Engineer), James Bulley, Fred Pocock and Ned Sparks.*
(Below) *Mrs. Ward, the tollgate keeper at Rye House, and Mr. Fred Smith, the Ware level-crossing keeper, who were featured in the BBC Radio programme "In Town Tonight" in November 1935.*

(Above) The Post Office staff in around 1900, posing outside the present Post Office which was built in 1893.   Before then the Post Office was situated at the northern end of the High Street building which is now Meadows' Grocery Store.
(Below) The Postmaster, Mr. J.W. Ashford, with a white beard, and the counter staff in 1897. Mr. Ashford was appointed Postmaster on the 1st July 1870 at a salary of £55 per annum.

Mr. Halfhide, an employee of the Beltona company, helping unload the mail at the rear of Amwell House in the 1930's.

(Above) Mr. Bob Maynard and employees of Maynard's Nursery in around 1920. This nursery was one of many which stood where the 100 Acre housing estate stands today.
(Below) Employees of Stevens' Nursery in the late 1930's.

Planting out, probably in one of the greenhouses of Mr. MacFarlane's Pitfield Nursery, in Nursery Road. The Kelly's Directory for 1945 lists a dozen nurseries in the Ware and Stanstead roads alone and by 1950 Hoddesdon was one of the main centres of market gardening in the Lea Valley. After the Second World War, many Italian immigrants were employed in the greenhouses and many went on to rent or own their own nurseries, and to succeed in other local businesses. In the past 15 years, competition from European imported vegetables and salads has led to a rapid decline in the industry. A number of nurseries do survive within the old boundaries of Hoddesdon U.D.C., but there are none in Hoddesdon itself.

(Above) Rye House watercress beds in the 1930's. The beds were started by James Welch and taken over by his son, Ernie. The business ceased virtually overnight when the water level fell during the Second World War.

(Below) The watercress beds of Mr. A. Hughes, which were established at the Lynch in 1885 and taken over by Mr. Walter Paddick in 1902. In the background can be seen the Lynch Mill, pulled down in 1892.

Another view of the Rye House watercress beds. The water was very good for growing watercress and the owner, Mr. Welch, also supplied willows to Sams of Hoddesdon, who made cricket bats and rackets.

ST. MONICA'S PRIORY, HODDESDEN, (HERTS). FRONT VIEW

Rawdon House photographed in 1960 when it was still occupied by nuns of the Order of St. Augustine. The house was built in 1622 by Marmaduke Rawdon, who was a wine trader in the City of London.

The Big House

The majority of the large houses in the High Street were built at the southern end of the town. This area, originally in Broxbourne Parish, was one where land was readily available and allowed the space for larger gardens.

Rawdon House was the earliest of these big houses and it must have dominated the southern end of Hoddesdon, when it was built in 1622. It was followed by the Grange, Yew House, Lowewood, Sherbourne House and Woodlands, as well as a number of smaller houses. Many of these have since been demolished and their sites developed or - as in the case of Rawdon House and the Grange - their magnificent gardens have been built upon. In the centre of the town, however, some of the larger houses survive. Among these are Hogges Hall, parts of which date from the 15th century, Stanboroughs, which is now the Conservative Club, and Rathmore House.

(Opposite) In common with many of the large houses in the town, Rawdon House had exceptionally fine gardens - now occupied by flats. This photograph, taken in 1891 by Bedford Lemere, is from the fine collection concerning Rawdon House owned by the Royal Commission on the Historical Monuments of England.

The entrance hall of Rawdon House in 1891 (another photograph from the R.C.H.M. collection). At the time, the house was owned by Henry K. Ricardo who had added the north wing in 1879. C.P. Christie became the owner after the Ricardos left Hoddesdon in 1892. Many of the 17th century fittings and several fireplaces were removed when the house was again sold in 1898 and became St. Monica's Priory.

Another superb interior of Rawdon House from the R.C.H.M. collection. The Rawdon family lived in the house for just over a hundred years until 1740 and it was then let to tenants for some years. Among these was John Dymoke, Hereditary Champion of England, but he stayed for only one year. Through the centuries, the house has had a number of names, including Hoddesdon House and Hoddesdon Great House, and has been a school as well as a Priory. Unlikely as it now seems, plans were put forward to demolish Rawdon House in 1969.

(Above) *The south face of High Leigh which was built for Mr. Charles Webb in 1851.*
(Below) *In 1871, the house was purchased by Mr. Robert Barclay who named it High Leigh. He made many improvements to the house and grounds, including the laying out of Barclay Park, which the Barclay family gave to Hoddesdon U.D.C. in 1935. Robert Barclay was a great benefactor of the town.*

(Above) *High Leigh, photographed in 1935 by which time it was owned by "The First Conference Estates Ltd.," and used as a conference centre.*
(Below) *The north front of High Leigh in about 1930.*

(Above) The Grange was built on the site of an old inn called the Cock. The earliest part of the house dates from 1657 when Marmaduke, second son of Sir Marmaduke Rawdon of Rawdon House, built a new house on the site. This view is of the west front, seen down the avenue which ran from the gates on Park View.

(Above) The east front of the Grange in the early 1930's, when it was the home of Mr. and Mrs. Tuke Taylor.

(Below) In 1725 the Grange was owned by Lady Arabella Oxenden, daughter of Lord Rockingham. She carried out a number of alterations, of which the fine iron gates and piers are still very prominent. In the scrollwork over the gates, Lady Arabella's monogram appears and this was at one time surmounted by a griffin's head, the Rockingham crest.

(Above) Today this building is known as the Spinning Wheel, but when built in 1870 by Septimus Warner it was known as "the Italian Cottage".
(Below) The Knowle in Cock Lane also dates from around 1870. This is a postcard view of the house in 1905.

Hoddesdonbury, a timber-framed building dating in part from the 16th century, probably marks the site of the old Manor House. In Domesday Book it was taxed as holding two hides and three virgates (about 300 acres). From 1242 until 1494 it was owned by members of the Bassingbourne family. Sir William Cecil acquired the manor in 1566 and his successors, the Salisburys, held it until 1800, when it was sold to Jacob Bosanquet of Broxbournebury. The house was re-fronted in the 19th century and was at one time the residence of Lady Maud Tree, the Edwardian actress.

(Above) Woodlands on the point of being demolished in 1967. This house dated from about 1830 and was built by the Quaker John Warner.

(Below) The early 19th century orangery, built by John Warner in the grounds of Woodlands. He created beautiful gardens on the twelve acres of land to the south and west of the house, including terraces, serpentine walks, plantations, shrubberies, dells, caves and artificial ruins, all carefully tended by an army of gardeners.

(Above) Little Woodlands was built as the stables of John Warner's house in 1833, and is now a private house.   Note the 19th century granary on the right.
(Below) The gothic lodge to the Woodlands Estate, as it was in 1958.

(Above) The rear of Hogges Hall at 64 High Street. This house underwent many changes in the mid-19th century which altered its appearance. The two northern bays are timber-framed of the 15th century.

(Below) An interior view of Hogges Hall in about 1925.

Lowewood is a Georgian town house, built in 1760, although parts of it may be from an earlier building.   The three Misses Warner (Harriette, Mary and Celia) lived here for many years: they were the unmarried daughters of John Warner and his second wife, Sarah.   In 1936 it was given to the town by Mr. Douglas Taylor for use as a public library.   It is now the home of both the Borough of Broxbourne Museum, which was officially opened on the 2nd July 1982, and also the Broxbourne Arts Centre.

St. Katherine's Chapel in a print of circa 1800. Its last recorded use for services was in 1706.

Hoddesdon at Prayer

Worship in Hoddesdon was for many centuries a complicated business, with the town split unevenly between the parishes of Great Amwell and Broxbourne. A chapel in honour of St. Katherine was built in 1336 by one William de la Marche, described as the King's Cook. He obtained the grant of a certain vacant space in Hoddesdon "so that he may build anew a chapel", which seems to suggest that there was an earlier building. The new chapel stood on the site now occupied by the clock tower and was situated in Amwell parish. There were many disputes with Broxbourne over this chapel. It would appear from parish records that inhabitants of that part of Hoddesdon which was in Amwell parish had to obtain special leave to use Broxbourne Church, and were rarely allowed burial there.

Hoddesdon did not become a separate ecclesiastical district until 1844. The present parish church had its origins in the chapel built by Robert Plomer in 1732. This was extended in 1865, with a bell tower and spire added in 1887. The Church of St. Cuthbert in Rye Park was consecrated in 1908 to serve the growing population of that part of the town.

Until 1932, Roman Catholics in Hoddesdon formed part of the Catholic Parish of Hertford, although from 1898 they were under the immediate charge of the chaplain of St. Monica's Priory, located in Rawdon House. Many other religious bodies have worshipped in the town, the oldest probably being the Society of Friends (Quakers) in 1683, followed by the Congregationalists towards the end of the 18th century. In the 19th century, the Baptists and Methodists became established in the town.

(Right) Another print of St. Katherine's Chapel. In 1700 one of the bells was removed from the old chapel and sold to provide a new clock. The remaining bell, which is still in the present Clock Tower, served as a "curfew bell" and was rung on royal birthdays and on Shrove Tuesday. The old chapel was pulled down in 1835.

(Below) An engraving of 1850, showing the chapel built in 1732 by Robert Plomer. This building now forms the nave of the Hoddesdon Parish Church.

(Above) The parish church as it looked before 1887 when the tower was built. The building on the right was purchased in about 1850 for use as a vicarage. It was pulled down when the present vicarage was built in 1895.
(Below) The interior of the parish church in around 1905. It was altered and modernised in 1976.

Hoddesdon Church.

A view of Hoddesdon Parish Church in 1905. The chapel built by Robert Plomer fell into disuse after his death in 1742 and it was not until the early 1820's that the building was purchased from its owner, Captain Hugh Hughes, and restored. It was consecrated as "the Chapel of Hoddesdon" on the 8th July 1823 by John Hawley, Bishop of London, who five years later became Archbishop of Canterbury and crowned Queen Victoria in 1837. The chapel was extended in 1865 and the bell tower was added in 1887. A peal of eight bells was donated by the Christie family in 1901. The church was re-dedicated as the Parish Church of St. Catherine and St. Paul on the 25th November 1976.

NEW INDEPENDENT CHAPEL,

(Above) The architect's design for the Congregational Church which was built in 1846 on the site of the old George or St. George Inn. Most of the money to purchase the site was raised by the Revd. William Ellis and the church was opened on the 27th April 1847.

(Right) The Congregational Church just before the Second World War. The poster on the railings says: "Peace can be Negotiated, but never Dictated".

(Above) The interior of the Congregational Church in about 1960.   The last service was held on the 23rd July 1967 and shortly afterwards the church was demolished to clear the way for the development of Fawkon Walk.

(Below) Laying the foundation of the Baptist Church in Essex Road in 1914.

(Above) The Methodist Church in Middlefield Road, which was built in 1929. The Methodists had previously used a building in Roman Street and before that the Coffee Tavern Hall in Lord Street.

(Below) The old chapel of the Elim Pentecostal Church in Rye Road, shortly before its demolition in 1986.

St. Augustine's Roman Catholic Church was built on the site of Esdale House and the first service was held on the 5th August 1962. Esdale House, which was built in 1878 by the Christie family, had been purchased for the church in 1932 and a house of studies, known as St. Augustine's Priory, was established there.

(Above) The building of St. Cuthbert's Church in Whitley Road, Rye Park, was financed by Mr. Robert Barclay of High Leigh. Earlier services had taken place in St. Cuthbert's Hall in the Old Highway, a corrugated iron building since demolished. The new church was consecrated on the 29th December 1908.

(Below) The Society of Friends or Quaker Meeting House in Lord Street, which was opened in 1829.

The "Ware Road Room" or Gospel Hall, as it became known was attached to the back of Fourways House. It was used for worship by the Brethren, who broke away from the Congregational Union during the 19th century. When work began on the town's road improvements in 1974, the building was demolished. A number of bodies were removed from the small burial ground and re-interred in Hoddesdon Cemetery on Ware Road.

A large crowd gathered outside the Bull Hotel for Queen Victoria's Diamond Jubilee in 1897.

Great Events

In common with most towns in Britain, Hoddesdon has seen the celebration of many great national and local events. The area around the Clock Tower has figured prominently in photographs of these events, with the crowds gathered in front of the tower and spilling out into the roads on either side. Before its demolition in 1833, the Market House would have served as a convenient gathering point and the place where news of national and local importance was imparted to the townsfolk.

For the Golden Jubilee of Queen Victoria in June 1887, a public dinner was provided at midday in a special marquee erected for the occasion. This marquee was constructed of scaffold poles, covered by tarpaulins, and stood just to the south of the Clock Tower. In the afternoon there were sports, followed by a children's tea and, to complete the day's celebrations, a large bonfire was lit on Westhill. Ninety years later in 1977, another royal event was celebrated locally. This was, of course, the Silver Jubilee of Queen Elizabeth II. Fifteen years on, this too is now part of Hoddesdon's past.

The chairman of Hoddesdon Urban District Council, John Alfred Hunt (owner of the building firm) reading out the Proclamation of King Edward VII in 1901.

(Above) The Proclamation of King George V in 1910, following the death of his father, Edward VII, on the 6th May.
(Below) A parade of the Widows' Joy Lodge (Oddfellows) in about 1900. This was the town's first friendly society, established in 1847.

(Above) Another view of the Proclamation of King George V.
(Below) The Street outside the Swan and the Salisbury Arms lined by townsfolk, celebrating the Coronation of King George V on the 22nd June 1911.

The High Street decorated to celebrate the end of the First World War in 1918.

Unveiling of the Hoddesdon and Rye Park War Memorial on the 10th April 1921. Two days before the unveiling, the memorial was being lowered into place, when it crashed to the ground and was damaged. Hasty repairs were carried out and it was again lowered into place, this time without incident. However, it is some eight inches shorter than originally intended. On the 29th July 1951, two plaques bearing the names of 40 local men who lost their lives in the Second World War were dedicated by the Revd. Osborn.

The building on the left of the picture is Borham House, demolished in 1965.

Borham House was the scene of Hoddesdon's most notorious crime. It was here on the 20th October 1807 that Thomas Simmons wilfully murdered two women - Mrs. Esther Warner, the first wife of John Warner and daughter of Mr. and Mrs. Borham, and Mrs. Hummerstone, who was visiting Mrs. Borham. Simmons had been discouraged from courting one of Mrs. Borham's maids and in a fit of temper he forced his way into the house, brandishing a knife. He attacked all three women that he found inside and only Mrs. Borham survived.

He then ran from the house, knocking down old Mr. Thomas Borham who tried to stop him. A large crowd of men searched the town and found Simmons hiding in an outbuilding not far from the scene of the murder.

He was handcuffed and taken to Hertford Gaol. In March 1808, he was convicted of murder at Hertford Assizes and hanged.

(Above) Beating the Bounds in 1936. The first account of the ceremony is found in 1750, though the custom dates from at least Anglo-Saxon times. This photograph shows some of the participants outside the Fish and Eels at Dobbs Weir. Councillor W. Winsor is holding the banner, with the chairman of Hoddesdon U.D.C., Councillor A. Festing Bryant, next to him. On the right of the banner are Mr. C. Whitley, Mr. Philip Longmore and Mr. F.W. Mutton.

(Below) A gathering of local dignitaries at High Leigh in June 1935, when Hoddesdon U.D.C. acquired Barclay Park as the result of a Deed of Gift by Mr. R.L. Barclay on behalf of the Barclay family.

Crowds of townspeople line the High Street for the Victory Celebration and Parade in 1945, following the end of the Second World War.

The 1945 Victory Parade, with a march past of some of the Air Raid Wardens who served the town and district throughout the war.   A victory fête was also held at Lowfield on the 14th July 1945.

(Above) The comedian, Arthur Askey, opening the new Tudor Hall on the 11th February 1955. On his right are members of the Haward family which owned the building.

(Below) The results of the 1955 General Election being read out from the front of the Tudor Hall.

The official opening of the new Hoddesdon Urban District Council offices on the 21st December 1935, by Councillor R.W. Merchant, chairman of the council. The council offices had previously been accommodated at 60 - 62 High Street. New offices became necessary when the Urban District was enlarged earlier in 1935 to include Broxbourne and Wormley. Following the reorganisation of local government and the creation of the Borough of Broxbourne in 1974, new offices were built at Bishop's College, Cheshunt and opened in 1986. The Hoddesdon offices, including those in the picture, were then sold off.

The sad sight of the Maidenhead, one of Hoddesdon's oldest inns, and the High Pavement properties in Amwell Street being demolished in 1964.

Demolition

When we look at Hoddesdon today, it is quite easy to overlook the fact that previous generations were quite adept at demolishing buildings. The Victorians in particular removed a number of buildings from the High Street during the second half of the 19th century. Charles Peter Christie used his undoubted influence to demolish three properties in 1877 and build for himself Esdale House. This was in turn demolished to make way for the present Catholic Church, less than one hundred years later.

However, it was during the 1960's and 1970's that Hoddesdon lost more buildings than at any time during its history. Many of these demolished buildings were familiar landmarks, such as the Bull Hotel, Yew House, Fourways House and the properties on the high pavement on the eastern side of Amwell Street. This latter group, together with the Maidenhead Public House and a number of Victorian cottages, was bulldozed in 1964 to clear the way for the Tower Centre development.

A HERON GROUP OF COMPANIES DEVELOPMENT

HODDESDON
TOWN CENTRE

An artist's impression of the Tower Centre, occupying the space cleared by demolition between Amwell and Burford Streets, from the Heron Group's brochure.

Work on the Tower Centre began in 1965 and in the Hoddesdon Journal of October 1966, the architect was quoted as saying: "The pedestrian courts in the development are to be treated in an interesting and artistic manner, and landscaping will be carried out as far as is practicable, including special lighting and seating to give pleasant surroundings in which shopping can be done in comfort."

Compare this picture with the view of just four years earlier, illustrated on page 19!

The old shops on the right of the picture were demolished in May 1955. The northernmost property had an archway, with a room above it, which led to the Common Marshes. The centre of the archway marked the former parish boundary between Broxbourne to the south and Great Amwell to the north. The Enfield and St. Albans Co-op Store now stands on the site and the old boundary is commemorated by a special paving stone in the footpath outside. In 1992, the building in the centre of the picture again became a shoe-shop when Burrs moved there from Fawkon Walk.

Paul's Lane in about 1956. Most of the properties on the left of Paul's Lane were demolished in 1958.

This picture shows the building which replaced the Bull Hotel.   It is now Gateway Foodmarkets.

The fate of the historic inn was sealed at a Local Inquiry on the 3rd October 1961, following which the Minister of Housing and Local Government agreed with his Inspector that "a suitably designed new building could replace the Bull without detriment to the street scene".   The late Ted Paddick, a local historian and at the time the town's Librarian, wrote in strong terms about the proposal: "Let those who have it in their power to act, see that we get a town of picturesque usefulness, and not one resembling a suburban planner's dream of dismal utilitarian uniformity".   The Bull was demolished in 1964 and the result was as shown above.

This block of buildings in the High Street was demolished in the early 1960's. At one time, it was an inn known as the Falcon on the Hoop, and by the late 17th century had become the Griffin. The archway led to Griffin Yard, which according to the Board of Health Report of 1851 was not the most hygienic place to live.

(Above) The Coffin House took its name from its coffin shape. It was demolished in 1959 despite efforts to save it, including a plea from Sir John Betjeman in his Daily Telegraph column "Men and Buildings". Today the site is occupied by the flats of Priory Close.

(Below) Old flint-faced cottages in Duke Street, photographed in around 1902.

A view of Yew House just before demolition.

There is no record of when Yew House was built but it contained traces of 17th century work. It was greatly altered in the early 19th century. In 1790, it was the home of Edward Christian, a barrister and later Professor of Law at the East India College at Haileybury, who was also the brother of Fletcher Christian, leader of the mutiny on H.M.S. Bounty in 1789. From 1802-32, Yew House was the home of Admiral W. Peere Williams and later of Admiral Donat Henchy O'Brien, who gave his name to Admiral's Walk. The house was sold on the 21st March 1962 and demolished soon afterwards. The site is now occupied by Cedar Green.

(Above) The old building known as "Graces" at the corner of Lord Street in 1877.

(Below) The old timber-framed building which adjoined the Maidenhead Inn, photographed in 1872. It was demolished in 1875.

Two views of Esdale House, which was demolished in 1961 to make way for the new Roman Catholic Church. The photograph above was taken from the High Street just before demolition, while that below is a view of the back of the house in 1910. Esdale House was built in 1878 for Charles Peter Christie, owner of the Hoddesdon Brewery.

(Above) Sherbourne House stood on part of the site later occupied by the Hoddesdon Motor Company.   It was demolished in 1965.

(Below) Large late Victorian houses on Parkview, awaiting demolition in 1975.

(Above) Houses on the east side of Amwell Street in the late 1950's.

(Left) Plume's Yard which lay directly behind the Maidenhead Inn. Access was from Burford Street.

Rye House Power Station began generating electricity in 1951 and was a familiar landmark for miles around. It closed in 1982 and was demolished in 1991 - 92.

Boys British School, Hoddesdon.
Published by A Norris

A print of the Boys' British School in Esdale Lane. It was built in 1841 by John Warner, but closed soon after the Boys' National School was opened in Paul's Lane in 1844. It is now the headquarters of the British Legion.

Schooldays

Early in the 19th century, Mrs. Easter Jones, a prominent local resident, built and endowed with £1,000 a Charity School for Girls in the Hamlet of Hoddesdon. This was the forerunner of a number of charitable and private educational establishments that provided a place of learning for the town's children during the last century.

In 1844, through the efforts of the first Vicar of Hoddesdon, the Revd. R.W. Morice, a Boys' National School and a Master's House were built at the west end of Paul's Lane. This was made possible by voluntary subscriptions and grants. Later that year the Infants' National School was provided by subscriptions. As a result of these events, the Nonconformist British School for Boys, established in Esdale Lane in 1842, closed but a Girls' British School was built in 1847 alongside the newly-constructed Congregational Church.

It was not until 1880, when the Education Act of 1870 was amended, that school attendance was made compulsory up to the age of ten. However, elementary education had to be paid for and school fees were not abolished until 1891. These fees varied from a penny (1d.) to fourpence (4d.) a week and many families could ill afford to lose the earnings and help of their children, let alone to pay for them to go to school. Some protested by attacking teachers!

(Above) A class of the Girls' National School, Paul's Lane, in about 1900.

(Below) The Girls' National School in 1930. The teacher is Miss Saward.

(Above) Playtime at the Paul's Lane schools. The building on the left was first occupied by the Girls' School in 1858. In 1900 all the local schools assembled in the Market Place in honour of Queen Victoria's birthday. A short service took place before the schoolchildren marched around the town in procession, accompanied by two bands.

(Below) A mixed class at the Paul's Lane school in around 1948. The Junior Mixed and Infants Schools remained at Paul's Lane until 1953, when the juniors moved to Haslewood School in Burford Street. The infants moved to a new school on the Haslewood site in 1971. Shortly afterwards the old school buildings were demolished to enable the entrance to Paul's Lane to be widened.

(Above) Rye Park School, Walton Road, was opened in 1909. This photograph was taken on the 21st October 1948.

(Below) Another class of pupils at Rye Park School, this time in 1946. The school originally catered only for juniors, but in 1933 the National School in Rumbold Road closed and the infants moved to the Walton Road site.

(Above) *Pupils at the Hoddesdon Secondary Modern School, Burford Street, with their teacher, Miss Giddens, in June 1951.*
(Below) *Haslewood School, Burford Street, which was opened in 1930.*

Pupils at the Hoddesdon Secondary Modern School at the school's open day in 1950, when they prepared a Wedding Breakfast and dressed up accordingly.

(Above) An aerial view of Haslewood School in about 1935. It was known as Burford Street Senior County Council School until 1948.

(Below) The new secondary modern school in Stanstead Road, now the John Warner School, just before its opening in September 1952.

HODDESDON TOWN FOOTBALL CLUB
SEASON 1935-36
Winners of Spartan League Division I and Dunkels Memorial Cup. Holders of Perry Charity Cup

Mr. W. PLUMPTON  Hon. Secretary & Treasurer

Back Row—H. MOORE, R. W. MERCHANT (*Chairman*), A. J. SAMS (*Vice-Chairman*), W. R. STONE, H. THURGILL, J. PAYNE, J. MEEKS (*Groundsman*).
Middle Row—J. OLIVER, W. BLAXILL, R. BARTHOLOMEW, S. STOKES, J. BINKS (*Vice-Capt.*), J. CAMERON, J. W. BOWLES, F. CLARKE,
W. J. BROOKS (*Auditor*), T. KNIGHT, A. YOUNG.
Front Row—P. A. JONES (*Assist. Sec.*), A. WARREN, L. SMITH, C. MARTIN (*Capt.*), J. W. GREEN, W. G. HAYNES, F. CHALKLEY (*Trainer*).

Hoddesdon Town Football Club in the 1935 - 36 season when they were winners of the Spartan League Division 1, the Dunkels Memorial Cup and the Perry Charity Cup.

Hoddesdon at Play

The decades following the 1860's saw the rise of organised sport in this country and, for once, it was something which filtered down to the working classes. Sports, such as football, cricket, swimming and athletics, became very popular and were participated in and enjoyed by rich and poor alike.

Hoddesdon Town Football Club is the second oldest club in Hertfordshire, having been founded in 1879. The cricket club was formed in 1882 and played organised matches on Lowfield, by kind permission of Robert Barclay. The town was also fortunate when towards the end of the 19th century the first public covered swimming baths in the county - and possibly in the country - were erected alongside Christie's Brewery, warmed by water from the brewery itself.

However, enjoyment of leisure was not confined to sporting activities and in the 1890's the invention of the wireless, gramophone and cinema heralded the arrival of new and exciting pursuits.

(Above) Hoddesdon Town F.C. in 1920 - 21. The club started life as Hoddesdon F.C. on a pitch in Mancers Field and changed to Hoddesdon Town when they moved to the club's present ground at Lowfield. The club's greatest achievement was in 1975 when they became the first side to win the F.A. Challenge Vase at Wembley.

(Below) As well as the Town, many junior football teams were established in Hoddesdon. This is the Rye Park Football Club in about 1900.

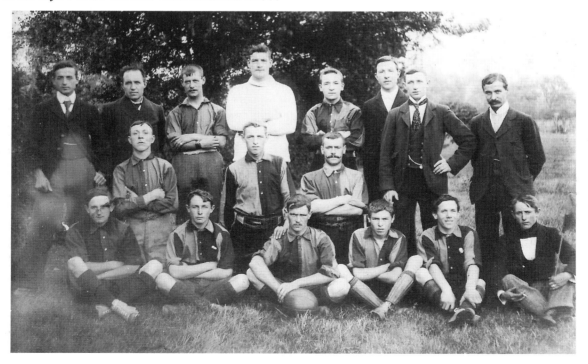

(Above) Members of the Hoddesdon Harriers Athletic Club, pictured outside the old pavilion at Lowfield Sports Ground.
(Below) Hoddesdon Cricket Club in 1890.

(Above) The Hoddesdon Silver Prize Band in 1922.   The non-playing gentlemen are from left to right: Tom Davies, C.A. Christie, F.C. Port and E. Dixon. The band, which was formed in 1902, earned the right to call themselves a prize band when they won a contest at Hertford in 1922.

(Below) Members of the Hoddesdon Institute which won first prize at the town carnival in 1912.

Hoddesdon Swimming Club

AFFILIATED TO S.C.A.S.A. AND R.L.S.S.

President - CHAS. A. CHRISTIE, ESQ.

PROGRAMME OF

SWIMMING GALA

AT THE BATHS, HODDESDON

(By kind permission of Messrs. Christie & Co., Ltd.)

On Thursday, Sept. 23rd, 1926, at 7 p.m.

Referee—CHARLES A. CHRISTIE, ESQ., J.P.

Judges—TOM E. DAVIES, ESQ., J.P., F. C. PORT, ESQ.,
E. D. ALLEN, ESQ., G. B. CHRISTIE, ESQ.

Starter—MR. R. W. MERCHANT.

Time-keeper—MR. ALEC YOUNG.

Stewards—Messrs. C. W. BLAXILL, S. CURTIS, J. ELSEY,
H. HACKETT, H. F. HAYLLAR, G. JEFFREYS, F. W. KENT,
T. KNIGHT.

Lady Stewards—MISS BROWN, MRS. KENT, MISS SAWARD.

Whips—Messrs. G. EDWARDS and W. STONE.

Hon. Secs.—Messrs. R. W. MERCHANT and W. R. STONE.

Hon. Treas.—MR. C. J. ROSS.

Handicapping has been done by a Committee of 6 members.

The PRIZES will be distributed immediately after each event by

MRS. CHAS. A. CHRISTIE

NOTICE TO COMPETITORS.

All Competitors must be ready to start in their respective Races at the specified time.
Any Competitor starting before his number is called will be disqualified.
The Committee reserve the right to alter this Programme as they may deem necessary.

PROGRAMME :: :: :: :: **TWOPENCE**

Knight & Co., Printers, Hoddesdon

*The front cover of the programme for the Hoddesdon Swimming Club Gala at the Brewery Baths,
Bell Lane in 1926.*

(Above)   A river carnival at the Fish and Eels, Dobbs Weir, on the 11th July 1912.

(Below)   A lorry decorated by supporters of the People's Dispensary for Sick Animals and sponsored by Mr. Franklin's Hoddesdon Newsreel, in the carnival of 1953.   The driver is the author's father, Mr. "Ginger" Dent.

Hoddesdon Cinema was opened on the 15th March 1913 by a company headed by a Mr. Hatrick, thereby stopping a rival scheme proposed by the proprietor of the Ware Picture House to build a cinema in Duke Street. It closed in 1930 and became the Robert Gilling Hall in 1949. This picture of it was taken in 1924 when the Territorials were holding a recruitment drive.

The Pavilion Cinema opened on the 3rd February 1930, incorporating part of the former buildings of Christie's Brewery. It was on the Shipman and King circuit and originally had seating for 838 patrons. It also had dressing rooms and facilities for storing scenery, thus making it possible to put on limited stage shows. On the 4th September 1933, cinemagoers were introduced to a new attraction, a "Christie 3c/6" organ, but whether this name had anything to do with the former brewery is not known. The Pavilion closed in 1972 and became a Bingo Hall.

Engraved by John Rye, from a Drawing by J.C.Smith.   For the Beauties of England and Wales E.W.B del.

THE RYE HOUSE,
Hertfordshire.

An engraving of the old gatehouse at Rye House, made for the book "The Beauties of England and Wales" in 1807.

In 1443, Sir Andrew Ogard was granted a licence by Henry VI to "impark and fortify the Maner of Rye". The gatehouse is all that remains of the house that Ogard built, and it is one of the earliest examples in the county of the re-introduction of brick into building. The house achieved notoriety through the Rye House plot to murder Charles II and his brother, James Duke of York, on their way back from the races at Newmarket in 1683. The then owner of Rye House, Richard Rumbold, was implicated in the plot which was foiled when the King returned to London earlier than expected.

During the late 18th and early 19th centuries, the gatehouse was used as the Parish Workhouse of Stanstead Abbotts. In recent years, it has been extensively restored and opened to the public by the Lee Valley Regional Park Authority.

RYE HOUSE HOTEL.
A. J. VINCE, Proprietor.

Photo. by T. S. Robinson, Homerton.

(Above) The Rye House Hotel in about 1925. The earliest record of this riverside inn is found in 1756, when it was known as the King's Arms.
(Below) A view of the Hotel from the river in about 1900.

Ye Rye House Hotel

(Above) *The Retainers' Hall, which was in fact a converted malting. The Rye House Estate was leased in the 1840's by Henry Teale, who set about turning it into a showplace with all manner of attractions. When Teale died in 1876, a local paper said: "For many years past, Whit Monday at the Rye House has been a noted day - from 20 to 25,000 being there generally and 600 to 800 vehicles".*

(Below) *The Great Bed of Ware was one of the popular attractions. Teale purchased it for 100 guineas in 1870 from the Saracen's Head Inn in Ware. The bed is now in the Victoria and Albert Museum, London.*

BALL ROOM & CONSERVATORY.

THE

PALAIS - DE - DANSE

OF

HERTFORDSHIRE.

FITTED THROUGHOUT WITH ELECTRIC LIGHT, CLOAK ROOMS AND ALL MODERN CONVENIENCES.

A MAGNIFICENT FLOOR.

This Ball Room can be Hired for Private Parties Visiting Rye House on Reasonable Terms for which, Please Apply to the PROPRIETOR.

One of the pages from the Historical Guide to Rye House, which could be purchased by visitors. The attractions there continued to draw the crowds even after the First World War, but not in the same numbers. By the 1930's it had become run-down.

On the 8th and 9th May 1924, a Grand Fête and Pageant was held in the grounds of Rye House to raise money for the Rye Park and District Infant Welfare Centre, which had recently been built in Rye Road. The opening ceremony was performed by H.R.H. Princess Arthur of Connaught.

(Above) A scene from the pageant with the Retainers' Hall in the background.

(Below) Mrs. Brooks, whose husband owned the ironmongery business in Hoddesdon High Street, played the part of the wife of King Henry VI in the opening episode of the pageant.

A group of local Air Raid Wardens photographed in Murchison Road during the Second World War.

Hoddesdon People

The photographs in this final chapter are not linked by any common theme, nor by a specific period in Hoddesdon's past. However, they do convey the wide variety of people who have lived here and given something of themselves to Hoddesdon - whether in times of peace or war, or in times of change or contentment and pleasure.

Richard Simmons (1775-1862) was the Parish Beadle for Broxbourne and the Postman for Hoddesdon. He was a well-known local character who had fought in the Battle of Waterloo in 1815.

John Warner, the Quaker who built Woodlands, was influential in the town for much of the early 19th century. He financed the construction of the Boys' British School in Esdale Lane.

(Above) A street party in Whitley Road to celebrate the end of the Second World War in 1945.

(Below) The inaugural meeting of the Hoddesdon Society at the Esdale Hall on the 15th September 1961. Left to right: Mr. E. Thompson, Mr. E. Bartleet, Mr. E.W. Paddick, Mr. A. Bartleet, Mrs. E. Thompson, Captain I. McCleod, Mrs McCleod and Councillor L. Jones.

(Above) Nursing staff and local mums with their children outside the Rye Park and District Welfare Centre in Rye Road in the late 1920's.
(Below) Councillor Hastings, the last chairman of Hoddesdon U.D.C., with 12 former chairmen and one chairwoman, Mrs. Dutton, photographed in 1974 when the council merged with Cheshunt U.D.C. to become the Borough of Broxbourne.

In 1622, water was supplied to the newly built Rawdon House from Godes Well Acre, near what is now High Leigh.   Finding he had more water than he needed, Sir Marmaduke Rawdon in 1631 laid a pipe from his house to a point in the High Street close to Conduit Lane.   There he set up the figure of the Samaritan Woman with the water pouring from her pitcher into a small pond.   In 1826, the disfigured statue was removed and replaced by an iron pump.   The statue languished at the rear of a property on the west side of the High Street until 1894, when a plan was put forward to re-erect her in the High Street.   Nothing came of this, and it was not until 1937 that the Samaritan Woman was re-erected behind the new council offices.   When these were sold in 1986, the statue was moved to the garden of Lowewood House, by then the borough museum.

Index